an infatuation

Lesbian Portraits

by Rose Collis
Illustrations by Ekaterini Harvey

M·Q·P

In the early 1990s, the mainstream media finally discovered that, in the words of a famous slogan, 'lesbians are everywhere'. But, as we shall see, passionate love between women is no modern social phenomenon – it has existed as long as women themselves, whatever term has been used to describe it. Lesbians have been 'inverts' and 'female adventurers', women who are 'not as other women' and who participate in 'romantic friendships' or 'Boston marriages', which supposedly consist of little more than holding hands and reading poetry to each other. The cultural influence of lesbians has been seen in every field, from social and political reform to art and literature. Yet historians have repeatedly failed to record the contributions made by these women. And, contrary to popular belief, lesbians throughout ancient and modern history have often been subjected to persecution similar to that of gay men. In 15th- and 16th-century Europe, women were executed for 'marrying' other women. Many of those burned during witch-hunts were women who chose to live without men.

The Roman collection of the British Museum in London includes a tombstone that had marked a double grave. At first sight, it appeared that the couple buried in the tomb were a man and a woman; the position and markings on the figures indicating that they had been married. On closer inspection, however, it was obvious that both had originally been female. Someone in the ancient world - or at the time of excavation - had crudely altered certain features on the face and torso of the right-hand figure so that it looked more masculine. The perpetrator, obviously outraged by this evidence of love between women in times of antiquity, took it upon themselves to tamper with history.

Notes

Lesbian history and culture is as old as the hills. But conventional wisdom throughout the centuries has continually pointed to Sappho, one of the ancient world's great lyric poets, as being the first recognisable lesbian figure - though not without argument. The more traditionally-minded scholars of her work - though conceding that she was a Lesbian - have continually questioned whether she was a lesbian. Confused? So were they! One translator of her work in the 1960s decided 'that she was temperamentally, at least, a sexual invert seems possible. That she was a pervert, there is no way of telling.'

Prejudices, it seems, are timeless. Ho-hum. Nonetheless, whenever women have euphemistically been described as having 'Sapphic inclinations', the meaning has been clear, as shown in this nudge-nudge, wink-wink verse penned by the French writer Clement Marot some 2000 years after Sappho's death:

> Among these virgins
> There are quite a few
> Who in morals resemble Sappho
> More than in sense.

What we do know about Sappho is that she lived in the 6th century BC and was born in Eressos on the island of Lesbos. She was briefly married, had a daughter called Cleis, and came from a wealthy family. Many of her songs were written about young women of Lesbos from similarly refined backgrounds. The exact date and manner of Sappho's death are, like most of her life, steeped in legend and folklore. One popular theory was that she loved a young boatman, Phaon, and, when he spurned her, she threw herself from a cliff - this conveniently ignores the fact that Phaon was mythological character! The few poems and fragments of Sappho's work that have survived, including the following example, bear a different interpretation altogether.

Notes

Notes

I think no girl
That sees the sun
Will ever equal you in skill

Pretty One, I'm yours again
far too long apart

Your beauty, your dress thrills all those who
see you
And the heart in my breast quickens;

(19th century translation)

Much of Sappho's poetry was destroyed. The Christians burned her poems when in AD390 they purged the Great Library at Alexandria, - the depository for works by all the great writers of the ancient world. In the 11th century, Pope Gregory VII ordered her remaining writings to be publicly burned. But excavations in Egypt between 1897 and 1906 unearthed the Oxyrhynchus Papyri, which were found to contain many fragments of Sappho's poems. Greek scholars maintain, nevertheless, that less than a twentieth of her work has survived.

Notes

Notes

In 1928, the French writer Pierre Louys caused a ripple of excitement when he claimed to have discovered *Les Chansons de Bilitis*, a book of erotic prose poems, supposedly written by a female contemporary of Sappho. Louys said he had translated them from the ancient Greek and even included a potted biography of Bilitis. He did manage to fool a great many people for some considerable period - thus perpetrating one of the great literary hoaxes of all time. Louys had actually written *Les Chansons* himself and the character of Bilitis was equally fictional. The episode did show how interest in, and enthusiasm for, Sappho continued unabated.

But long before Sappho ever put pen to parchment, her home island was briefly populated by a famously strong tribe of women; the Libyan Amazons. They invaded Lesbos, not to mention Syria, Egypt, Algeria and north-west Africa. In February 1997, an excavation in the Russian steppes unearthed a number of women's graves, dating back as far as BC600, containing daggers and long swords, which archaeologists believe prove that the Amazons had lived around the Black Sea - a claim originally made by the historian, Herodotus. Legend has it that the Libyan Amazons used to remove their right breasts so that they could fight with more freedom. Ouch! The Amazons' traditional weapon - the double-bladed axe known as a 'labrys' - was adopted by lesbians in the latter half of the 20th century as a symbol of strength and pride.

Notes

Notes

Did Ruth and Naomi 'know' each other in the biblical sense? Naomi's husband, Elimelech, died and she and her widowed daughter-in-law, Ruth, went to live in Bethlehem together. Naomi tried to dissuade Ruth from the journey – Ruth's passionate answer has become a popular declaration of love, often used in heterosexual marriage ceremonies:

Entreat me not to leave you or to return from
following you;
For whither thou goest, I will go
Where thou lodgest, I will lodge
Thy people shall be my people, and thy God my
God:
Where thou diest, will I die, and there will I be
buried:
The Lord do so to me, and more also,
If aught but death part thee and me.

Book of Ruth, 1:16–17

To G, her one and only rose,
Her A this bond of true love shows.

When I recall how you caressed
So joyously, my little breast
I want to die.

Anonymous, 12th century

St Teresa of Avila lived in 16th century Spain, and founded 20 convents which adhered to the strictest rules of separatism. But in a biography of Teresa, *The Eagle and the Dove* (1943), it emerged that Teresa had been in love with one of her young female cousins. Her biographer happened to be Vita Sackville-West, of whom more later.

Notes

Notes

Another nun, Benedetta Carlini, was born in Tuscany, in Italy, during the Renaissance. Documents which were not discovered until the 1980s by historian Judith Brown detailed Benedetta's passionate and secret relationship with another nun. The love affair was discovered and Benedetta spent the last 35 years of her life in prison.

The modern image of Sweden's Queen Christina, who ruled in the 17th century, is one of great beauty and glamour, courtesy of Greta Garbo's portrayal in the 1933 movie. Contemporary reports, however, speak of the Queen being rather squat and afflicted with facial pock marks. Nonetheless, she was blessed with a remarkably rebellious attitude. Raised as a boy by her father, Christina abdicated in 1654, rather than agree to her ministers' demands that she marry and bear heirs to the throne. Her loves included Angelica Georgini, an opera singer, and the Countess Ebba Sparre, who left her after the abdication.

Notes

Notes

Queen Anne of England, far from relinquishing her hold on the crown, did everything in her power to hang on to it, despite her appaling health, made considerably worse by her 17 pregnancies from her marriage to Prince George of Denmark. Her commitment to her domain was only matched by her devotion to her friend, Sarah, Duchess of Marlborough. 'Nothing but death can ever make me part with you. For if it be possible, I am every day more and more yours', Anne once wrote to her beloved. The two women first met when they were children. 'She even then expressed a particular fondness for me', said Sarah. And, despite their respective marriages - Sarah wed the ambitious and highly successful military campaigner John Churchill - 'This inclination increased with our years.'

Sarah's affections were outweighed by her ambitions for her family, however, and she fell out with the ailing Queen. Anne switched her affections to Abigail Hill, one of Sarah's cousins and a former Woman of the Royal Bedchamber. This ditty was written anonymously about them in the early 18th century:

When as Queen Anne of great Renown
Great Britain's Scepter sway'd
Besides the Church, she dearly lov'd
A Dirty Chamber-Maid

Her Secretary she was not
Because she could not write
But had the Conduct and the care
Of some dark Deeds at Night

In 1721, an extraordinary trial took place in the town of Halberstadt, Germany. Two women, Catherina Linck and Catherina Muhlhahn, were put on trial for sodomy. Linck had masqueraded as a man for many years - devising an uncanny set of male genitalia for herself - serving as a soldier with the Hanoverian and Royal Prussian troops. In 1717 she met and married Muhlhahn but the couple fell out. Muhlhahn's mother forced her to admit to the authorities that Linck was not a man. Linck was condemned under an archaic, Church-based 13th-century law which decreed that lesbian sex was equivalent to male sodomy - the punishment for which was death. Catherina Muhlhahn was sentenced to three years' imprisonment and exile.

Notes

In Daniel Defoe's bawdy novel *Moll Flanders*, our heroine links up in London with a skilled pickpocket, Lucy Diver, who tells her, 'I never cared for any man the way I cared for you'. Sadly, just a few days after declaring her love for Moll, Lucy is arrested for theft and condemned to the gallows. 'Lucy pleaded her belly but to no avail', says a desolate Moll. 'For she had lain with none but me these several months.'

Notes

I therefore with tears entreated her to go to bed.
She reply'd,
Most willingly my soul, if you'll go with me.

Helen Williams, *Anecdotes of a Convent*, Vol. 1, 1771

In the 18th century, newspapers began to take a great interest in 'romantic friendships' between women, which were dismissed as an 'unnatural vice'. The focus of much of this attention were the Ladies of Llangollen, Lady Eleanor Butler and Sarah Ponsonby, two women of similar Irish gentry backgrounds who outraged their families and society by 'eloping' to Wales in 1778. There they set up house together, with a servant known as 'Molly the Bruiser' (the three women now rest in the same tomb) and lived happily ever after, until death did them part, more than 50 years later. Subsequent attempts to desexualise their association failed miserably when Eleanor's coded journals were deciphered and published, and contained clear evidence of a physical relationship.

Anne Lister, mistress of Shibden Hall in Yorkshire in the early 19th century, left written evidence of her sexuality. In a secret journal, not discovered and decoded until the 1980s, she chronicled her affairs with women, some of whom were married. She was also a mistress of quaint euphemism, notably 'queer' (her term for the female sexual organ), 'grubbling' (meaning a type of lovemaking) and 'gone to Italy', which meant having a full sexual relationship.

Notes

The French artist Rosa Bonheur (1822-1899) achieved huge acclaim for her animal portraiture, but she was equally known for her mode of dress and her infamous put-downs of the male sex. 'Oh dear sir, if you only knew how little I care for your sex, you wouldn't get such queer ideas into your head. The fact is, in the way of males, I like only the bulls I paint', she once said.

Bonheur secured a special permit from the police – a *permission de travestissement* – which allowed her to wear men's clothing in public places. This did lead to some confusion, though. One policeman tried to arrest her because he thought she was a man impersonating a woman! Bonheur shared her life with two women, firstly Natalie Michas, and then the young painter Anna Klumpke. The three women are buried together in the Père Lachaise cemetery in Paris.

Notes

In 1811, two private school mistresses in Scotland found themselves accused of 'grubbling' – indeed, as Anne Lister might have put it, of having gone as far as Italy. The accusation was levelled against Marianne Woods and Jane Pirie by one of their pupils, Jane Cumming. As a result, parents rapidly withdrew their daughters and the school collapsed. To clear their names, Marianne and Jane had to sue the girl's family, who had spread the story, for libel. After nearly ten years of legal wrangling, the teachers won their case and settled for damages out of court.

A Funny Valentine:

I'll send a kiss, for that would be
The quickest sent, the lightest borne,
And well I know tomorrow morn
She'll send it back again to me.

Notes

The poet Christina Rossetti was the subject of many works by her better-known brother, the artist Dante Gabriel. Her first book of poems was published when she was 32 but she suffered from poor health all her life. In her 40s, she contracted Graves' disease and then, 20 years later, cancer. She was engaged twice but did not marry, and some of her verse hints at her personal ambiguity. In *Winter: My Secret* (1857) she teasingly wrote:

> I tell my secret? No indeed, not I:
> Perhaps some day, who knows?
>
> You want to hear it? well:
> Only, my secret's mine, and I won't tell.

Her lengthy poem *Goblin Market* (1859) went further:

Golden head by golden head
Like two pigeons in one nest
Folded in each other's wings
They lay down in their curtained bed.

Cheek to cheek and breast to breast
Locked together in one nest.

Did you miss me?
Come and kiss me,
Never mind my bruises,
Hug me, kiss me, suck my juices,
Squeezed from goblin fruits for you,
Golden pulp and goblin dew
Eat me, drink me, love me
Laura, make much of me.

In 1873, Irish-born Frances Power Cobbe, journalist, philosopher, social reformer, women's rights campaigner, and pioneering anti-vivisectionist, penned her own passionate and – remarkably for the time – explicit 'Valentine' to her lifetime companion, Mary Lloyd:

Hereafter, when slow ebbs the tide
And age drains out my strength and pride
And dim-grown eyes and trembling hand
No longer list my soul's command
I'll want you, Mary.

In joy and grief, in good and ill,
Friend of my heart! I need you still,
My Playmate, Friend, Companion, Love,
To dwell with here, to clasp above
I want you, Mary.

Notes

While the lights were going out all over Europe, a curious all-female phenomenon was being created in Japan, which still thrives today. In 1914, entrepreneur Ichizo Kobayashi founded the Takarazuka Troupe, incorporating the drama of classical Japanese plays and the melodrama, fantasy and music of opera. Enrolled at 16, young women undergo a highly disciplined and regimented form of training before being assigned to one of the four Takarazuka troupes. Early on, a decision is made about whether they will play highly romanticised male or female roles and their training is then determined accordingly. The 'male' players are dressed and styled as young men, on and offstage, but their combination of heavy make-up and slickly coiffured hair looked, in the 1990s, like the epitome of 'lesbian chic'. Interestingly, audiences attending Takarazuka shows in Japan, which are always sold out, are virtually 100 per cent women.

Notes

When French writer Colette left her tyrannical first husband, she formed a relationship with the Marquise de Belboef, who dressed like an elegant young man and was known as 'Missy'. The pair caused a storm when they performed together in music hall shows in France, in which Missy played the male roles and kissed a near-nude Colette. One performance at the Moulin Rouge in 1906 was stopped by the police.

In pre-talkie Hollywood, the Russian-born actress Alla Nazimova had become the centre of a West Coast 'sewing circle' that included her lover, Natasha Rambova, designer and erstwhile wife of Rudolf Valentino. Nazimova caused a storm when she produced and starred in a screen version of Oscar Wilde's *Salome*, which featured an all-gay cast.

Notes

Notes

Another prominent woman in Hollywood's early days - and a figure in Nazimova's circle - was the gifted director Dorothy Arzner. Although not the only female film director at that time, Arzner was the most daring and well-known. Her films were gently subversive. *Christopher Strong*, starring Katharine Hepburn, and *Craig's Wife* were unusual critiques of conventional male/female relationships. *Dance, Girl, Dance* examined the lot of chorus girls and *The Wild Party* focused on a group of female college students. Arzner left Hollywood in 1943, and lived with her partner, fashion designer Marion Morgan, from the late '20s until Morgan's death in 1971. And they said it wouldn't last.

Spanish-born writer Mercedes De Acosta caused something of a stir amongst the Hollywood establishment when she went to work for RKO in the late '20s. She formed a relationship with Greta Garbo, who shocked studio bosses by adopting De Acosta's favoured mode of dress – trousers. 'Garbo In Pants!', blared one headline, and a photo of the two women walking down Hollywood Boulevard together in trousers was captioned 'Innocent bystanders gasped in amazement'.

Notes

Eva Le Galliene was the English-born actress who became the toast of Broadway and founded New York's acclaimed Civic Repertory Theater. Offstage, her lovers included Alla Nazimova and Mercedes De Acosta. In 1921, the eternally-glamourous Le Galliene surprised her fans by agreeing to model masculine sports clothes in *Theatre Magazine*.

Notes

The following year, theatre-goers in New York had the chance to see the first-ever lesbian love scene in English-language theatre. *The God of Vengeance* was written by Sholom Asch, the first Yiddish playwright to achieve wide recognition. Set in a Jewish brothel in Poland, the play's first act ended with a passionate embrace between two young women; Act Two contained a more explicit love scene. During its Broadway run, the play's entire cast and its producer were arrested and charged with violating the penal code which 'defines the crime of presenting an obscene, indecent, immoral and impure theatrical production'. They were eventually found guilty and given suspended sentences.

The American poet Amy Lowell was posthumously awarded the Pulitzer Prize in 1926. She wrote ten volumes of verse, including *Pictures of the Floating World* and *Ballads For Sale*. What was less well known during her lifetime was that many of the poems were inspired by her longtime partner, the actress Ada Russell, whom she dubbed 'Peter'.

You are ice and fire,
The touch of you burns my hands like snow.

(From *Opal*)

When you came, you were like red wine and honey,
And the taste of you burnt my mouth with its sweetness.

(From *Decade*)

Selma Lagerlof, the much-loved Swedish author, made history in 1909 when, at the age of 50, she became the first woman to win the Nobel Prize for Literature. Her work drew on Scandinavian legends, myths and folklore. One of her best-known works, *Gosta Berling's Saga*, was made into a film, starring Greta Garbo. Selma shared most of her adult life with her partner, Sophie Elkan, who died in 1921. Vita Sackville-West once said of Selma that 'She writes always as a woman; not one of her books could have been written by a man'.

Notes

Don't forget your toothbrush! Dame Ethel Smyth, the English composer, writer and suffragist, could have testified to the wisdom of this advice. In 1910, Smyth was introduced to Emmeline Pankhurst, founder of the Women's Social and Political Union, and pledged to commit two years of her life to furthering 'the cause'. Her first act was to compose *March of the Women*, which became the suffragettes' theme tune. 'Every great cause needs a tune,' she told Pankhurst. 'A thumping great march!'

Notes

During a stone-throwing attack on the house of Britain's Colonial Secretary, Smyth and Pankhurst were arrested. Sentenced to ten months' imprisonment, the women were put in adjacent cells in Holloway Prison. When the next influx of convicted suffragettes were being marched up the stairs to their cells, they started to sing *March of the Women*, at which Ethel grabbed her toothbrush, poked her arms out of her cell bars and conducted them. Ethel Smyth's devotion to women also included passions for Lisl von Herzongenberg, Virginia Woolf and Emmeline Pankhurst herself.

Notes

Edy Craig, actress, producer and daughter of the theatre legend Ellen Terry, also became involved in the fight for women's suffrage. Edy didn't join the WSPU but the more radical Women's Freedom League, whose focus was on direct action, rather than parliamentary progress. She also belonged to the Actresses' Franchise League and organised fund-raising shows for the WFL. Edy's lifetime partner was the novelist and playwright Christopher St John, and their home in London became a 'safe house' for suffragettes hiding from the police.

The two women lived next door to Ellen Terry in the Kent village of Smallhythe. Eventually, their relationship became triangular when they were joined by the painter Clare 'Tony' Atwood. Edy's nicknames for Chris and Clare were 'Master Baby' and 'The Brat'.

While the fight for women's rights was gathering pace, a remarkable and unique community of women, involved in writing, publishing and art, was gradually settling on the Left Bank in Paris. It was started by American heiress Natalie Barney at the turn of the century and ended only when the Nazis invaded Paris in June 1940. Most of the women were either lesbian or bisexual, and many formed professional and personal partnerships that lasted for decades. Such a recognisable, geographically-defined cultural female community was rare and, up to the present day, has not been repeated.

Notes

Notes

It began after Natalie Barney and her then lover, the English poet René Vivien, travelled to Lesbos at the turn of the century to set up a lesbian school based on Sappho's philosophies of beauty, sensuality and freedom. When her plans fell apart, Barney simply decided to choose a different location for her community: Paris. Coming from a background of inherited wealth, Barney was able to buy a large house on the Left Bank and, for the next 60 years, her 'salons' attracted not just notable female personalities, including Colette, Gertrude Stein and Edith Sitwell, but their male contemporaries, like Jean Cocteau, André Gide and Thornton Wilder.

Barney was not known as 'L'Amazone' for nothing. Throughout her life - even when she was in her 90s - she continued to woo and win an impressive succession of lovers. They included Dolly Wilde, niece of Oscar, who apparently not only resembled her uncle physically but also shared his gift for writing. Barney said she was 'half androgyne and half goddess'. Unfortunately, Dolly was unable to harness her talents, preferring just to startle people with her witty and charismatic personality.

Natalie Barney's lifetime partner was the American painter Romaine Brooks. One of Brooks' best-known paintings, *La France Croisée* (1914), a portrait of a Red Cross nurse, became a symbol of France at war. Her relationship with Barney continued for 55 years - and they said it wouldn't last! Incredibly, though, it didn't endure until death. Brooks finally lost patience with her famously non-monogamous lover in 1968, when they were in their 80s, after Barney fell in love with diplomat's wife Janet Lahovary. Brooks ended the relationship and refused to speak to Barney again.

The Left Bank women also included Janet Flanner, whose influential and acclaimed '*Letter From Paris*' appeared in the *New Yorker* for over 40 years; the photographer Berenice Abbott; and Jane Heap and Margaret Anderson, founders of the highly influential literary periodical, *The Little Review*, (particularly important in its promotion of ex-pat writers).

One of the most enduring and outstanding partnerships involved Sylvia Beach, the American founder of the English language bookshop Shakespeare & Co, in Paris. She was also the first publisher, in 1922, of James Joyce's *Ulysses*, championing the Irish writer's work at her own expense when no established publisher would. Her lifetime partner was Adrienne Monnier, who in 1915 opened the bookshop La Maison des Amis des Livres, which subsequently became the centre of the French Anglo-American intellectual and literary circle.

Notes

Notes

In 1928, Djuna Barnes – another leading woman of the Left Bank – published a privately-printed, satirical book called *Ladies Almanack*, under a pseudonym. It contained thinly disguised portraits of many of Paris's leading lesbians. Natalie Barney was Dame Evangeline Musset, a lesbian 'missionary', out to 'recruit'. Romaine Brooks was Cynic Sal and Radclyffe Hall was Tilly Tweed-in-Blood. *Ladies Almanack* was just one of more than 500 novels with lesbian content published 1875–1940.

In 1928, another infamous piece of lesbian fiction was published – but with far greater impact and, subsequently, immeasurable influence. Radclyffe Hall was a moderately respected writer, as well known for her masculine, be-monocled appearance, whose novel *Adam's Breed* had won several literary awards. But it was *The Well of Loneliness* which brought its author into the public eye. It is, when all is said and done, a stodgily written, rather tame account of the loves of a young woman, Stephen Gordon, who, in the book's language, is an 'invert'. The only reference to sex was contained in one sentence, which has become one of the best-known erotic euphemisms of all time: 'And that night they were not divided'. The book was dedicated to 'Our Three Selves', a reference to Hall, her longtime partner, Lady Una Troubridge, and the late Mabel Batten, Hall's first love.

Notes

Notes

When it was sprung on the great British public, however, *The Well of Loneliness* prompted a torrent of abuse. 'I would rather give a healthy boy or girl a phial of prussic acid than this book', said James Douglas in the *Sunday Express*. A copy of the book was sent to the Director of Public Prosecutions and, in August 1928, the Home Secretary banned it. Copies, printed in France, were seized by police when they arrived in Dover; and 287 copies were destroyed in the furnaces at Scotland Yard. The ban was not lifted until 1958, 15 years after Radclyffe Hall's death. Interestingly, the American authorities did not adopt such a censorious attitude and the book's publication did much to bring the existence of lesbians out into the open.

While the mainly white women of the Left Bank were making such an impact in Paris, lesbian and bisexual black women were making a significant contribution to America's jazz and, in particular, what was known as the 'Harlem Renaissance'. Bessie Smith – dubbed 'Queen of the Blues' – brought the musical genre out of its roots in the rural South and became its most popular proponent. Although married to Jack Gee, Bessie spent a good deal of her time 'in the life' – that is, enjoying relationships with other women. She might have claimed that she didn't understand 'mannish acting women' in *Foolish Man Blues* but it sure didn't fool those in the know.

Notes

One of Bessie's contemporaries was the singer Ma Rainey, whose best known song, *Prove It On Me Blues*, is still regarded as a gay classic. In it, Rainey sings boldly about going out with her friends, who must have been women 'cos I don't like no men', and admits that 'I wear a collar and a tie'.

Another leading Harlem figure was jazz singer Gladys Bentley, who at 16 had run away from Philadelphia to seek fame, fortune and acceptance in New York. She sang and played piano at bars and parties in Harlem's underworld before getting her big break as featured entertainer at the Mad House Club, and she also played piano at the famous Cotton Club. Bentley - often resplendent in tweed suits or white tuxedo - became one of the best-known black female entertainers in America during the 1920s. Dressed in men's clothes, she went off to Atlantic City to marry her girlfriend. But, after the Depression, Bentley's world began to crumble. In 1940, a nightclub had to apply for a special permit for her 'to wear trousers, instead of skirts' in her act. During the '50s, in the repressive atmosphere of McCarthy's anti-gay purges, Bentley started wearing dresses, had hormone 'treatment', wrote an article, 'I Am a Woman Again', in *Ebony*, in which she rejected her lesbianism and, in a last-ditch effort to save her career, married a man 16 years her junior.

In 1929, a warrant was issued for the arrest of a Colonel Barker, who had failed to attend his bankruptcy hearing – on the face of it, a trivial news item. However, it soon emerged that the 'Colonel' was Lilias Arkell-Smith – alias 'Victor Barker' – who had been passing herself off as an Army officer for years. But the real surprise was that, as Victor Barker, she had married a young woman called Elfrida Haward in a Brighton church in 1923. She was charged with perjury and with making a false statement in a marriage register and, in court. Elfrida abandoned her, claiming she had no idea her husband was a woman. Arkell-Smith was found guilty and sentenced to nine months imprisonment. In the '30s, she re-emerged as the centrepiece of a sideshow in Blackpool, then disappeared from public view until she sold her story to a Sunday paper in the '50s.

They all wrote fiction but none of them could have come up with storylines that matched the events of their real lives for complexity, intensity and unconventionality. 'They' were the three Vs: Vita Sackville-West, novelist, poet, gardener, traveller, and wife of the British diplomat and writer, Harold Nicolson; Violet Trefusis, socialite and writer, daughter of Alice Keppel, the mistress of King Edward VII; and Virginia Woolf, the novelist, essayist, and diarist, whose frail mental health eventually led to her suicide.

Vita and Violet had first met as children. Their love affair blossomed in 1919 after Vita had been married to Nicolson for six years and had had two sons. Violet herself was married to Denys Trefusis. Much to the horror of both their families, the two women decided to elope to France. They spent several months together in Paris and Monte Carlo, where Vita sometimes passed herself off as a male character, 'Julian'. Eventually, after scenes of high emotion and melodrama, Nicolson persuaded his wife to leave Violet. But the passion between the two women was never truly resolved. After she returned to England, Vita kept her distance from Violet, knowing full well that their love was not so much an ember but an eternal flame, constantly flickering away. Instead, she poured her passion into her writing and into creating the world-famous garden at Sissinghurst.

Notes

There was, however, a third passion in her life: Virginia Woolf. Like Vita, the troubled writer enjoyed a marriage with her husband that was based on deep bonds of affection and loyalty, but without sexual passion. The two women first met in 1922 and their relationship – less stormy than Vita's affair with Violet – continued until Virginia's suicide in 1941. In 1927, Virginia began work on *Orlando*, her novel featuring an androgynous character who changes sex halfway through, which was written as the ultimate gift of love to Vita. Her youngest son called it 'the longest and most charming love-letter in literature'.

The perennial argument about whether a relationship between two women was an old-fashioned 'romantic friendship' or a fully fledged romance always flares up between opposing sides whenever 'evidence' is discovered that sheds new light on the sexuality of a famous woman. A case in point is the relationship between First Lady Eleanor Roosevelt, wife of legendary President Franklin D Roosevelt, and journalist Lorena Hickok. The Roosevelts enjoyed a relatively happy marriage, until Eleanor discovered her husband was having a passionate and intense affair with the woman who was her social secretary. Not long afterwards, she met Hickok. Their subsequent relationship was dismissed by the Roosevelt family and Eleanor's official biographer as 'romantic friendship', nothing more.

The truth is a little more complex. During the '30s, Lorena secretly lived at the White House with Eleanor for more than four years. And, more than 20 years after Eleanor's death, the correspondence between the two women rather contradicts the 'official' view. 'Oh! I want to put my arms around you, I ache to hold you close', Eleanor wrote to Lorena. 'Your ring is a great comfort. I look at it and think she does love me or I wouldn't be wearing it!'

Actress Tallulah Bankhead created headlines on both sides of the Atlantic, as much for her tempestuous offstage performances as her memorable film and theatre roles. Her public and indiscriminate fondness for drink, drugs and sex meant she cut a shocking figure in the '20s and '30s although, in later years, her behaviour became rather predictable and boring. But in her heyday, no-one could make jaws drop better than the switch-hitting Tallulah. On one occasion, she sashayed up to Joan Crawford, then married to Douglas Fairbanks Jnr, and declared, 'Darling, you're divine. I've had an affair with your husband. You'll be next.'

On screen in '30s Hollywood, a new trend seemed to be emerging - screen goddesses who were popping up in roles where they wore the pants and got to kiss the girls. And - surprise, surprise - the two icons doing this had been lovers of Mercedes De Acosta!

In *Morocco* (1930), Marlene Dietrich appeared as a cabaret performer who, clad in top hat and tails, first gives a rose, and then a smacking kiss, to a woman in the audience, to much ooh-ing and ah-ing.

Notes

Three years later, Greta Garbo fulfilled a long-held ambition by portraying Queen Christina. Although, in true Hollywood fashion, the film's central romance was between the male-attired Christina and diplomat Antonio (John Gilbert), early scenes touch on the Queen's relationship with Countess Ebba Sparre. They share an intimate kiss during one scene and, when Christina promises to see her that night, Ebba complains, 'You'll be surrounded by musty old men and musty old papers, and I won't be able to get near you'.

One of the most popular painters of English society during the '20s and '30s was Hannah Gluckstein, who preferred to be known by the androgynous moniker of 'Gluck'. Her stylish landscapes, portraits and self-portraits sold well throughout the '30s and she patented the 'Gluck Frame' - 'instead of the outer edge dominating, it was made to die away into the wall and cease to be a separate feature', she explained. Nesta Oberman was her lover for nearly ten years, which Gluck called the 'You We' period. 'We are not an affair - we are husband and wife,' she said of the relationship. One of her most famous portraits, *Medallion*, is a picture of herself and Nesta, which accurately reflects the inferiority she always felt in her relationships. Gluck was also painted by Romaine Brooks, in a portrait entitled *Peter, A Young English Girl*.

The work of Mexican artist Frida Kahlo – with their vibrant colours and stark images – couldn't have been more of a contrast to Gluck's stylish, restrained pictures. Kahlo's main subject was herself – her life and her pain. Aged 18, Kahlo was nearly killed in a freak tram accident. Her injuries, and the 30 operations she subsequently endured, left her bed-ridden and immobile for much of her short life. Though Frida was married to the famous Mexican muralist Diego Rivera, his last mistress, Dolores Olmedo, has said, 'It's public knowledge that she had more relationships with women than men'. But, as Raquel Tibol, one of her biographers, explained, 'People close to Frida deny she was bisexual'.

The pink triangle became a familiar gay symbol in the 1970s and '80s – gay men sent to concentration camps by the Nazis were made to wear this emblem on their prison uniforms. But a lesser-known symbol was the black triangle. Lesbians sent to the camps by the Nazi regime – usually on false charges of 'treason' or 'subversion' – were made to wear this emblem, which signified 'anti-social'.

Notes

Notes

One of those who succeeded in escaping from Nazi Germany was Erica Mann, daughter of the novelist Thomas Mann. In 1935, the poet W H Auden was asked a strange favour by his friend Christopher Isherwood: would he marry Erica so that she could get a British passport? Auden sent a one-word telegram in reply: 'Delighted'. Mann left Germany and she and Auden remained married until her death in 1969 - though, of course, they always continued to lead separate lives, shared with their respective same-sex lovers.

Another German lesbian who was growing increasingly aware of the dangers of fascism was the writer Christa Winsloe. Her 1931 play, *The Child Manuela,* was set in a turn-of the century school for the daughters of Prussian army officers. The story of Manuela's love for her teacher, Fräulein von Bernburg, was interpreted by some as a metaphor for the increasingly repressive atmosphere in Germany. Two screen versions were made of the play: Leontine Sagan's classic *Mädchen in Uniform* (1931) and *Schoolgirls in Uniform* (1958). Christa Winsloe and her lover, the Swiss writer Simone Gentet, worked for the French Resistance during World War II, hiding refugees in their house. Both women are believed to have been murdered by fascists in 1944.

Notes

Notes

Another key lesbian-themed play from this period - based on the real-life libel case of the Misses Pirie and Woods - also inspired two movies. The film rights to Lillian Hellman's controversial and award-winning *The Children's Hour* were bought by producer Sam Goldwyn. When someone told him it was about lesbians, he is alleged to have said, 'We can always call them Bulgarians'. Hellman adapted her own play for William Wyler's 1936 screen version called *These Three*.

During the 1930s, the multi-racial, all-woman jazz band The International Sweethearts of Rhythm toured America, to great acclaim. One of their trumpet players was Tiny Davis, the female Louis Armstrong of the time. When the group disbanded, she formed her own group, Tiny Davis and her Hell-Divers. Playing drums, bass and piano in the Hell-Divers was Ruby Lucas, Tiny's lover. A documentary was made about the pair in 1986, by which time they'd been together 43 years.

In rural England, a group of women began an experiment, dismissed at the time as 'cranky', which, perhaps if it had been thought of by a group of men, might have been more acceptable. Lady Eve Balfour was a niece of British Prime Minister Arthur Balfour. She studied agriculture and trained land army girls during WWI. By the late '30s, Eve was running a farm with her sister Mary, and her partner, 'Bel' Bearden. She decided to turn the farm into a research project, dedicated solely to organic farming research. Out of Eve's project came the founding of the Soil Association and the modern organic farming movement. Oh, and did we forget to mention? Eve lived with her partner, Kathleen Carnley, for 50 years, had 'worn trousers since the First World War when she discovered the freedom of breeches' and 'very sensibly, she chooses male slippers for comfort'.

Meanwhile, with the onset of WWII, women on both sides of the Atlantic were responding to the call to arms. The popular novelist and broadcaster Naomi 'Mickie' Jacob returned from Italy, where she had been living, and joined ENSA, the entertainment corps of the British armed forces. A lifelong opponent of fascism, Mickie had nearly fallen out with her great friend, Radclyffe Hall, when she discovered that one of Hall's lovers, Evugenia Souline, had pronounced anti-Semitic views. 'I disliked her with the utmost cordiality', explained Mickie. Her own lovers included the music hall star Marguerite Broadfoote.

Notes

Notes

Johnnie Phelps, a sergeant in the WACS, was hardly at ease when her commanding officer – who just happened to be General Dwight Eisenhower – ordered her to root out all the lesbians in her battalion. According to Phelps, that meant about 97 per cent of them. Displaying immense courage in the face of enemy fire, Phelps told him, 'If the General pleases, I'll be happy to do this investigation for you, but you have to know that the first name on the list will be mine'. At which point, another WAC in the room said, 'Sir, you must be aware that Sergeant Phelps's name will be second, but mine will be first'. Phelps continued, 'I think the General should be aware that among those women are some of the most highly decorated women of the war. There have been no cases of misconduct and, as a matter of fact, every six months the General has awarded us a commendation for meritorious service'. Eisenhower said, 'Forget the order'. Phelps later recalled, 'It was a good battalion to be in!'

Incidentally, while being a lesbian has never been against the law in the US or Britain, it is still, at the time of writing, classed as an offence in the armed forces. In Britain, any woman serving in the Army, Navy or Air Force can be charged with 'committing disgraceful conduct of an indecent kind which results in discharge'.

Notes

During the Nazi occupation of France, the controversial writer Gertrude Stein and her lifelong partner, secretary and representative on Earth, Alice B Toklas, moved to Paris to their country house at Bilignin. Meagre rations meant that Alice was not able to cook many of the dishes she had discovered during her long years in France though, during WWI, she had discovered some of her favourites. One was for Flaming Peaches, 'a simple and tasty dessert':

Flaming Peaches

Take six peaches (preferably fresh), cover them with boiling water for a few minutes, and then peel them.

Poach them in a little water, over a low heat, for three minutes. Put them in a heat-resistant dish, add a few ounces of sugar and a liberal measure of peach brandy.

Heat the syrup until nearly boiling and then ladle it over the peaches. Serve each peach alight.

Stein and Toklas survived the war, only for Stein to die of cancer in 1946 – their relationship had lasted nearly 40 years. Alice survived her lover for more than 20 years. At her death, she was buried alongside Stein in Paris's famous Père Lachaise cemetery. However, in death as in life, she decreed Stein should take centre-stage – her own inscription was put on the back of their joint tombstone, so only Stein's can be seen from the pathway.

Notes

A year later, one of America's best-loved writers, the Pulitzer Prize-winning Willa Cather – author of *My Antonia* and *Death Comes to the Archbishop* – died. At her request, all her remaining personal papers were burned. Years earlier, Cather had destroyed all her correspondence with Isabelle McClung, the woman with whom she had a relationship for 15 years.

Also in 1947, a woman who went by the name of 'Lisa Ben' – an anagram of 'lesbian' – created *Vice Versa*, the first American magazine produced specifically for lesbians.

Notes

In 1958, the world's first known organisation for lesbians, the Daughters of Bilitis, was founded by Del Martin and Phyllis Lyon in America. The group took its name from Pierre Louys' infamous book, *Les Chansons de Bilitis*. Martin and Lyon met in 1949 when they were both working for the same publisher in Seattle, their relationship began in 1953.

Naturally, once a lesbian organisation was in existence, its members needed a companion publication. *The Ladder*, a monthly magazine, was launched by the DOB in 1956, continuing publication until 1972.

Also in 1955, a quiet revolution occurred in the hitherto cosy world of women's magazines: *She* was launched onto an unsuspecting world – in more senses than one. The magazine's editor was Joan Werner Laurie and its main contributor was Britain's best-known female media personality, Nancy Spain. What most *She* readers were unaware of was that Joan and Nancy had been a couple since 1950 and were raising two sons in what was, for the time, a remarkably publicly avowed 'pretend family'. Nancy's flamboyant, show-off articles, coupled with Joan's steady, astute editing, made *She* the women's magazine that broke the mould and paved the way for the likes of *Cosmopolitan* and *Marie Claire*. By a strange quirk of fate, Nancy and Joan died together in a plane crash in 1964.

SHE
SHE

During its existence, *The Ladder* became a God-send to lesbians throughout America, many of whom were isolated in small towns. The magazine's letters' page became a forum for debate and discussion and one of its anonymous correspondents was black playwright Lorraine Hansberry. In 1958, she became the first black writer to have a play produced on Broadway with *A Raisin in the Sun*. Although married, Hansberry sent numerous letters to *The Ladder*, in which she declared that being a lesbian was a political choice. Sadly, she did not live to see how widespread this 'political choice' was to be – she died in 1965.

Notes

If lesbians had a theme tune at this time, it would surely have been the 1954 hit, *Secret Love*, by Doris Day. What song during the 1950s better – and more unwittingly – expressed the feelings that so many lesbians had to keep hidden 'within the heart of me'?

The Ladder was a step up from most of the reading matter that concerned itself with lesbians. Between 1950 and 1965, America's 'dime novel' paperbacks sold in their millions and, amongst the thousands of titles, were many on lesbian themes – not all of them written with the best intentions. These could easily be identified by their titles: *The Unashamed: Warped Desires of Women Who Need No Men*, *The Twisted Ones*, *Ladder of Flesh* (*A Story that Exposes Broadway as The Gay Way*) and, perhaps the best of all, *The Devil is a Lesbian*.

However, amongst all the trash could be found a number of books that actually had been written by lesbians, for lesbians. They included Vin Parker's *Spring Fire*, which was published by a mainstream house, Fawcett Gold Medal, in 1952. This was long after drink and drugs had caught up with the author, who had died penniless in London in 1941.

The Brinker books – now considered minor lesbian 'pulp' classics – continue to be best-sellers, right up through the 1990s. They were kept in print by The Naiad Press, the world's first lesbian publishing company, founded by Barbara Grier, a collector of lesbian literature and former editor of *The Ladder*.

Notes

Meanwhile, Mary Renault, the English-born historical novelist who lived most of her life in South Africa with her lover, Julie Mullard, was tackling gay male themes in her books. Set in the masculine military world of ancient Greece, *The Charioteer*, *The King Must Die* and *Fire From Heaven* became bestsellers. Her only lesbian-themed novel was *The Middle Mist*, which was originally titled *The Friendly Young Ladies*, but Renault's publishers, concerned about how sexually explicit her books were becoming, toned it down.

In 1964, Esme Langley founded Britain's first organisation for lesbians, the euphemistically-titled Minorities Research Group (MRG). As with the Daughters of Bilitis, MRG realised that its members desperately needed their own publication – and so *Arena Three* (or *A3*, as it became known) was created. One of its readers was Mary Renault, who wrote to Langley and MRG, praising 'the high and decent plane on which you are consistently keeping the whole subject'.

Notes

Arena Three and MRG metamorphosised into *Sappho* magazine and social group in the early 1970s, under the steady hand of Jackie Forster, one of the best-known lesbians in Britain. Forster had been friends with Nancy Spain during the '50s, although she was then married. 'I didn't have a clue what was going on,' she said later. 'I was straighter than the Fosse Way at the time!' Owing to financial difficulties, *Sappho* magazine finally ceased publication in 1981 but the social group continued into the 1990s.

In 1965, the first known gay rights demonstration – held in protest against the US State Department's purge of homosexuals – was staged outside the White House. One of the participants was Barbara Gittings from Philadelphia, who founded the New York branch of the Daughters of Bilitis. Gittings still had vivid memories of the first meeting of DOB she attended in San Francisco: 'I was in a room with 12 other lesbians for the first time, and oh, what a thrill that was!'

Notes

Notes

By the mid-'60s, the mountains of trashy lesbian pulp fiction were being countered by quality lesbian-themed books, written by authors with impeccable mainstream credentials. They included Jane Rule's *Desert of the Heart*; *Mrs Stevens Hears the Mermaids Singing* by the Belgian-born writer and poet May Sarton; Maureen Duffy's *The Microcosm*; *The Chinese Garden* by Rosemary Manning and, Isabel Miller's *Patience and Sarah*.

At last, lesbians had some quality reading matter to savour and could settle down with a good book and a nice tart - courtesy of Nancy Spain. In her *Colour Cookery Book*, she recommended a pear and cherry one:

Pear and Cherry Tart

Take four hard pears; peel, core and halve them.

Cook them with 4oz of sugar and half a pint of cider until slightly tender.

Drain the pears and arrange them with glacé cherries in a 9-inch baked pastry case.

Add half a pint of water to the cider. Heat this, then dissolve one packet of lemon jelly into it. Allow to cool slightly, then pour the liquid over the fruit. Leave to set.

Unfortunately, '60s film-makers were still serving up a steady diet of sour lesbian images. William Wyler's 1962 version of *The Children's Hour* - also known as *The Loudest Whisper* - starred Shirley Maclaine as the doomed Martha Dobie, who kills herself when her love for Karen Wright (Audrey Hepburn) is revealed. One of the most popular James Bond movies, *From Russia With Love* (1963) featured the legendary Lotte Lenya as Rosa Klebbe, a predatory butch lesbian whose stern Soviet uniform included shoes which boasted concealed spikes in the toecaps. And yes - you guessed it - she ends up dead, shot by the young woman she had previously tried to seduce.

Notes

Notes

One rare exception to the '60s cinema's portrayal of lesbians was Bryan Forbes' *The L-Shaped Room* (1962), about the residents of a downmarket London rooming house. Cicely Courtneidge played the house's oldest resident, a retired vaudeville performer who breaks into a song and dance routine at the drop of a hat. She makes frequent references to her 'friend', now dead, who she lived with for many years. 'A real love match, it was', she tells one of her house-mates. Eventually, she is asked about her friend – was 'he' a performer too? The old lady produces a framed photo of a woman, and gently explains, 'It takes all kinds you know, dearie'.

If only *The Killing of Sister George* could have had some of this sensitivity! Robert Aldrich's 1968 version of Frank Marcus's inoffensive comedy set back mainstream cinematic representation of lesbians for nearly 20 years. Beryl Reid's butchly bravura performance as the boozy, rebellious and overtly dykey soap actress, June 'George' Buckridge, won her many plaudits. However, the film's heavy-handed depiction of her abusive relationship with younger lover 'Childie' (Susannah York) succeeded only in reinforcing many of the old myths about lesbian stereotypes perpetuated by all those '50s dime novels. Even the film's 119-second seduction scene had 'trash' written all over it.

By this time, the gentle trilling of Doris Day's *Secret Love* had been usurped as a lesbian favourite by the raunchier sounds of the '60s. Lesbians were falling in love with Dusty Springfield declaring *I Only Want To Be With You* and responding to the sexy, earthy fusion of rock and blues screamed out by Janis Joplin. Joplin's unglamorous bisexuality touched a nerve with her female fans and it was no great surprise when, after her lonely death in October 1970 - from an overdose - the truth about her affairs with women was revealed. And, only two months before her own death, Janis had arranged for a headstone to be placed at the unmarked grave of her idol, Bessie Smith - another bisexual blues singer.

The '70s began with the publication of books which were ground-breaking studies of sexuality. *Love Between Women* and *Bisexuality: A Study* (1971) were both written by the acclaimed Dr Charlotte Wolff. During the 1930s, Wolff had fled from Nazi Germany, where she had been working in a family planning clinic, heading first for Paris and then London. Wolff wrote about her own relationships with women in her 1980 autobiography, *Hindsight*.

In 1970, American academic and feminist Kate Millett's *Sexual Politics* was published. She described the book, which had started life as her PhD dissertation, as 'notes towards a theory of patriarchy'. Predictably, male critics lambasted Millett and then the American feminist movement turned in on itself, with writer Betty Friedan denouncing lesbians involved in the fight for women's rights, singling out the-then bisexual Millett for particular criticism.

Notes

1973 saw the publication of one of the most enduring and endearing lesbian novels, Rita Mae Brown's hilarious *Rubyfruit Jungle.* It told the story of the romantic adventures of Molly Bolt, an uncompromising, outspoken and sassy Southern girl, raised by her tough foster mother. The book was originally published in America by Daughters Publishing Company, Inc, a tiny women's publishing collective. Within a few years, *Rubyfruit Jungle* was scooped up by a mainstream paperback house, Bantam Books, and subsequently sold over 300,000 copies. Rita Mae went on to further success with *Southern Discomfort* and *Sudden Death,* a tale of love and betrayal set in the women's tennis circuit and allegedly based on her relationship with one Martina Navratilova.

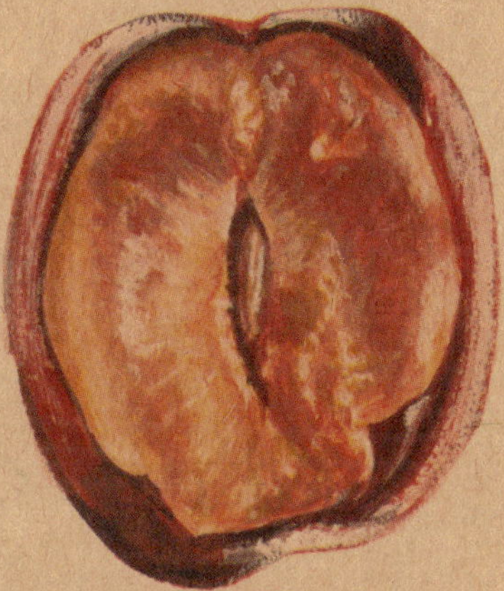

Notes

Other important lesbian writers of the time, whose writing dealt not only with sexuality but radical feminism and the fight against racism, included Judy Grahn, poet and academic, author of *The Words Of A Common Woman* and *Mother Tongue: Gay Words, Gay Worlds*, who had been dishonourably discharged from the US Air Force for being a lesbian; and poet Adrienne Rich, whose first collection, *A Change of World*, was chosen by W H Auden for the 1951 Yale Younger Poets Award. In 1973, Rich rejected a National Book Award for her collection, *Diving Into The Wreck*. Instead, she issued a joint statement with fellow nominees Audre Lorde and Alice Walker that she would only accept the award 'in the name of all women whose voices have gone and still go unheard in a patriarchal world'.

Audre Lorde, activist, writer, poet and professor, who died in 1992, was arguably one of the most important figures of this time – especially for black lesbians on both sides of the Atlantic, to whom it seemed that the predominantly white lesbian and feminist movements offered little alternative to racism and homophobia. Lorde had been on the 'gay-girl' scene in New York in the '50s. In the '60s, she married and had two children before, in 1963, meeting Frances Clayton, with whom she shared the rest of her life. In the '80s, Lorde published the books she became best known for, the autobiographical *Cancer Journals* and *Zami: A New Spelling Of My Name*, as well as editing the lesbian journal *Chrysalis* and co-founding The Kitchen Table – Women Of Color Press.

Notes

Notes

History was made in 1974 when Elaine Noble won election to the state legislature in Massachusetts, and became the first ever openly lesbian state representative in American history.

Out of the feminist movement in the early '70s came music that both reflected the movement and tried to provide an alternative to the mostly male-dominated commercial music industry, with varying results. The first 'women's music' album was *Lavender Jane Loves Women* (1974) by Alix Dobkin, Kay Gardner and Patches Attom, released on the Women's Wax Work label. This was soon followed by Meg Christian's *I Know You Know* (1974) from California-based Olivia Records, founded by Judy Dlugacz and other like-minded women. Christian and Cris Williamson became Olivia's mainstay artistes. Meanwhile, elsewhere in California, Holly Near – a stalwart of Jane Fonda and Donald Sutherland's 'Free The Army' anti-war shows in the early '70s – set up Redwood Records as an independent outlet for her work.

However, the squeaky-clean, wholesome sounds of Redwood and Olivia did not satisfy all tastes. As well as perennials like Dusty Springfield, cult lesbian favourites during the late '70s and early '80s included Gloria Gaynor's *I Will Survive* and *I Am What I Am* (actually a declaration of pride sung by a drag queen in the musical *La Cage Aux Folles*), the anthem-like *We Are Family* by Sister Sledge and *Love And Affection* – or just about any other track, in fact – by Joan Armatrading, fondly known as the 'Queen of the Bedsitters'. Punkier sounds came from the androgynous-looking New York performance poet Patti Smith and from Siouxsie and the Banshees.

French actress Maria Schneider had caused a sensation with her torrid scenes with co-star Marlon Brando in the 1972 shocker *Last Tango In Paris* – though rumours that the film inspired the advertising slogan 'I can't believe it's not butter' proved to be unfounded! Schneider inspired more tabloid headlines in 1975 when she took advantage of the 'right to be insane' and booked herself into a psychiatric institution in Rome, so she could be with her lover, American heiress Patty Townsend. Her film career has never been the same since.

Notes

Notes

In 1978, the now-defunct London-*Evening News* became the target of a number of direct action protests. The campaign was triggered off when the paper stooped to underhand tactics to produce a 'lesbian-shock-horror' story. Jackie Forster and other women connected with *Sappho* had been giving confidential, free advice to lesbian couples who wanted to have children by artificial insemination by donor (AID). The press got wind of this and sent along one of their female reporters to the group, posing as one half of a lesbian couple interested in AID. Having got all the information she needed – including the name of a sympathetic doctor – the reporter proceeded to write up a sensationalist story, headlined 'Dr Strange Love'.

A year later, came the British General Election which saw the rise of one woman politician – Margaret Thatcher – and the fall of another, Maureen Colquhoun, the member for the marginal Labour seat of Northampton North and, to date, the only out lesbian MP. Colquhoun, an outspoken advocate of women's rights and withdrawal of British troops from Northern Ireland, was married and a mother of three grown-up children when, in 1975, she met and fell in love with fellow feminist Babs Todd. Some of the more reactionary elements in her constituency party plotted to de-select her, though one maintained, 'Her sexual behaviour is not the issue'. Of course it wasn't! After a lengthy battle, she won the nomination to stand in the seat in 1979 but the national swing against Labour in the election meant that Colquhoun's slender majority disappeared. She remained active in local politics in London's East End before retiring.

Notes

Notes

Maureen Colquhoun paid the price for wearing her heart on her sleeve but, as the '80s progressed, more lesbians were choosing to wear their badges and buttons where they could be seen. The most popular slogans included 'Lesbians Ignite', 'How Dare You Presume I'm Heterosexual?', 'So Many Women, So Little Time' and (from an off-Broadway show), 'Vampire Lesbians Of Sodom'.

A grieving elephant called Moto brought a zoo to a standstill yesterday. She stood guard over the body of her elephant pal Toto, who had died of a heart attack, and refused to budge. They blocked the entrance to Colchester Zoo, Essex, forcing staff to shut out scores of visitors. The two she-elephants had been friends for 17 years. Zoo owner Angela Tropeano said: 'It is very sad. Toto was her only companion in life. She went into mourning immediately her friend died and just wouldn't leave her side.'

From the *Daily Mirror*, mid-1980s

In 1979, a time capsule was unearthed in San Francisco's Washington Square Park. It contained a copy of *The Great Geysers of California*, written by journalist Laura de Force Gordon. On the book's flyleaf, she had written 'If this little book should see the light of day after 100 years' entombment, I should like the readers to know that the author was a lover of her own sex and devoted the best years of her life in striving for the political equality of women'.

Notes

LESBIANS
ARE
EVERYWHERE!

During the '70s and '80s, lesbian slogans were coming off badges and ending up on walls and advertising billboards. Many of these were captured by the camera of Jill Posener, who was also responsible for writing the pioneering lesbian play, *Any Woman Can*, in 1975. Popular lesbian graffiti included 'Lesbianism – why settle for less?' and, an especially popular one, 'Lesbians Are Everywhere'.

The world of women's tennis was rocked to its foundations in 1981 when one of the greatest players in the modern game, Billie Jean King, was sued by her former lover, Marilyn Barnett, in a multi-million dollar 'palimony' case. Newspapers had first noticed Barnett when she was at Billie Jean's side during her 'Battle of the Sexes' match against Bobby Riggs in Houston in 1973. She claimed that their relationship had lasted seven years and that she was therefore entitled to half of Billie Jean's earnings during that time. At a press conference with her husband, Larry, alongside her, Billie Jean told reporters: 'I made a mistake. I am very shocked and disappointed that Marilyn has done this.'

Notes

Many mainstream TV critics failed to understand the appeal of the low-budget, high-rating Australian drama series, *Prisoner Cell Block H*, set in a women's prison. Two women from Derby, Roz Vecsey and Tracy Elliott, set up a fan club in honour of the programme which, they said at the time, contained 'the best portrayal of lesbians ever seen on the small screen'. *Prisoner* certainly had an infinitie variety of lesbian characters: Sharon Gilmore, cuddly Judy Bryant, Angela Jeffreys, leather glove-wearing sadist Joan 'The Freak' Ferguson and the old stone-butch herself, Frankie Doyle, who was shot by the 'bloody baaastards!' she was trying to escape from. Carol Burns, who played Frankie, said, 'She was wonderful – she was a very brave woman'.

The graffiti that Jill Posener captured on camera didn't focus on one single issue. Other popular slogans, including 'Dykes For Disarmament', reflected one of the biggest issues of the women's movement in Britain during the 1980s: Greenham Common. The Women's Peace camps were set up outside the US military base at Greenham in 1981, after Women For Life On Earth marched 125 miles from Cardiff to the base, in protest against the decision to deploy 96 Cruise missiles there. Other women's peace camps were set up at bases throughout Britain. Their inhabitants lived in tents, mud and 'benders' (made out of tree branches and plastic sheeting), endured verbal and physical abuse, evictions, fines and imprisonment. The Greenham women were often predictably dismissed as 'ugly, dirty lesbians' by their opponents. One woman quipped that, with all the evictions and actions, the chance to have a sex life would have been a fine thing.

Before *Prisoner Cell Block H* came along, lesbian viewers were glued to the female bonding evident in the hit police series, *Cagney and Lacey*, starring Tyne Daly as Mary Beth Lacey and Sharon Gless as Chris Cagney. The 1981 pilot starred Loretta Swit as Cagney, with Meg Foster taking over the role when it was developed into a series. However, ratings were disappointing and Foster was replaced with Sharon Gless. According to some press reports, the programme's producers thought that Foster's portrayal was a little too butch for viewers to take. One network executive apparently told the American magazine TV Guide, 'We perceived them as dykes'. Coincidentally, Foster had played a lesbian character in the 1978 movie *A Different Story.*

A Different Story was a well-meaning but confused stab at exploring alternative relationships - the story concerned the love affair between a gay man and a lesbian. *Personal Best* (1982) was a less well-meaning but equally muddled lesbian-themed movie, starring Mariel Hemingway and Patrice Donnelly as two Olympic athletes who have an affair. The relationship ends when Hemingway goes off with one of the guys.

Notes

Notes

John Sayles, whose intelligent and critically acclaimed films have included *Brother From Another Planet* and *Lone Star*, tackled the twin themes of coming out and lesbian custody in the low-budget feature *Lianna*. Though its toe-curling bar scenes and blue-lit, French-whispering sex scene were embarrassing, the film was firmly on the side of newly-out Lianna, whose spineless academic girlfriend leaves her at the end of the movie.

But the best lesbian movie to come out (pardon the pun) of the 1980s was Donna Dietch's *Desert Hearts* (1986), adapted from Jane Rule's classic story of love and choice, *Desert of the Heart*. Rule herself pronounced the movie 'a little miracle'. Helen Shaver and Patricia Charbonneau played repressed Evelyn and wild-gal Kay, whose love blossoms in the arid atmosphere of the desert outside divorce-capital Reno in the '50s. Dietch had to raise the film's finances independently over fours years and it was shot in 31 days. Helen Shaver told a reporter, 'We did it for love and all the peanut butter sandwiches we could eat!'

Notes

Notes

On 22 September, 1985, Europe's oldest lesbian club, The Gateways, in Chelsea, London, swung shut for the last time. It had been opened as a private drinking club by Ted Ware in 1945 and was taken over by his wife, Gina Ware, in the '50s. Under Gina's strict stewardship - aided by her business partner Smithy - the club built up a loyal following and, for many lesbians in those twilight days, it became their only way of meeting others. 'It's been part of so many of our lives', said one regular. The club achieved worldwide fame when it was featured in Robert Aldrich's notorious film, *The Killing of Sister George*; several scenes were shot in the club, and many of its regulars were used as extras.

In 1987, Margaret Thatcher's government decided to stop local councils in Britain 'promoting homosexuality' – in books, plays, films and art – by introducing Clause 28 of its new Local Government Act. This single clause mobilised the lesbian and gay communities throughout the UK and Europe like no single issue had ever previously done – and lesbians were in the forefront of action taken against it. In 1988, one group gained entry into the House of Lords, where the assembled peers were debating the Bill. When it was voted through, the women abseiled into the chamber in protest.

Notes

Notes

One of the women who had been active at Greenham was Annie King. In 1988, Annie and three other women staged one of the most daring pieces of lesbian activism in history. On the day that Clause 28 was due to become law, they gained access to the BBC television newsroom and chained and handcuffed themselves to the presenters' chairs, camera cables and anything else available. As the Six O'Clock News bulletin began, the four women shouted 'Stop the Clause' and 'Stop Section 28'. Annie King had handcuffed herself to the chair of newsreader Sue Lawley, who told viewers, 'We have rather been invaded'. The protest gained huge publicity for the 'Stop The Clause' campaign and produced one of the best tabloid newspaper headlines of all time: 'Beeb Man Sits on Lesbian'.

Tragically, seven years later, Annie King and her lover, Bel Rowe, were killed in an accident when they fell from cliffs near Srabster in the north of Scotland while out walking. Investigators said it was possible that one of the women had slipped and the other had died trying to save her.

Notes

In the 1990s, Jeanette Winterson enjoyed the dubious honour of being the first lesbian author since Gertrude Stein to declare her own genius. While her more immodest statements, actions and less successful books have somewhat blighted her reputation, there is not doubt about the quality or reputation of her first novel, *Oranges Are Not The Only Fruit* (1985). Largely autobiographical, the book drew on her unusual childhood, growing up as the adopted daughter of an overzealous Pentecostal mother in a small Lancashire town. The book won many awards and Winterson adapted it for television in 1990. The series went on to scoop numerous gongs.

Notes

In 1993, Martina Navratilova – arguably the best woman tennis players in the game's history – found herself suffering the same fate as her former doubles partner, Billie Jean King, when her ex-lover Judy Nelson took out a multi-million dollar 'palimony' lawsuit against her. The case ended up in court and in tears and, in a final ironic twist, Nelson announced that she was now living with Rita Mae Brown – Martina's ex. A year after the court case, Martina announced her retirement from full-time tennis and became involved in lesbian and gay rights campaigns. 'Until we get what we deserve, I'll be active,' she said.

In the early 1980s, Kathy Dawn Lang from Alberta, Canada, was dabbling in performance art. A decade on, as country singer k d lang, she dotzey-dozed to international stardom in the early '90s with her album *Ingenue*, featuring lyrics about her unrequited love for a married woman, and by posing on the cover of *Vanity Fair*, being 'shaved' by supermodel Cindy Crawford. It was hardly necessary to tell the world what had been apparent to many people anyway, but come out as a lesbian she did.

Notes

Postcards were starting to reflect the times a little more daringly. 'Dip Me In Honey And Throw Me To The Lesbians' became a popular greeting to have thrust through your letterbox.

Notes

Notes

Lesbian film-making took a significant step forward in 1994 with *Go Fish*, a low-budget, slightly experimental romantic comedy which was picked up by a commercial distributor and became one of the independent hits of the year. Its writer and director, Guinevere Turner and Rose Troche, said the idea for the film came to them in a bar, 'probably after beer number 12. We wanted to make a lesbian film, a happy film. We didn't want a crisis film and we wanted to represent a younger audience, instead of one woman in crisis.'

The mainstream media on both sides of the Atlantic suddenly became obsessed with the concepts of 'lesbian chic', 'lipstick lesbians' and 'designer dykes'. One story they couldn't leave alone was the ambiguous friendship between Sandra Bernhard, who played the vain lesbian Nancy in *Roseanne*, and gender-tease Madonna, an avid collector of works by Frida Kahlo and Tamara De Lempicka – coincidentally both bisexual. Madonna and Bernhard made high-profile public appearances together and flirted outrageously with each other on national TV. However, at some point, the friendship turned distinctly sour – some sources close to Bernhard claim it was because Madonna was stealing all her ideas – and the 'M' word became a taboo with Bernhard. Another taboo word for her is 'lesbian' – her resolute refusal to be labelled infuriated many of her gay fans and sections of the gay press. 'I just think I'm better than calling myself a 'gay performer' to placate the gay community because I'm not a gay performer,' she explained. 'I'm a universal performer.'

Notes

Notes

In the 1990s, British soap operas discovered the existence of lesbians. Suddenly, they all wanted to see what difference a gay made. In the '80s, *Brookside* and *EastEnders* had included a few fleeting cameo appearances by lesbian characters. But, as the concept of 'lesbian chic' filled the pages of the newspapers and magazines, so did it reach the soaps, who played it very safe by introducing characters who all had very long hair and, with one exception, were clumsily written out.

Notes

In *EastEnders*, things were less dramatic. No sooner had the sexuality of its lesbian couple – a barmaid and a hairdresser – been made apparent than they left Albert Square for sunnier climes. However, the series does (to date) include in its cast one of Britain's best-known lesbians – Pam St Clement, who plays the much-married Pat Beale/Wicks/Butcher/Evans.

Pam St Clement

Notes

When k d lang came out, it seemed to set off a chain reaction. In the mid-1990s, more women singers and musicians announced they were lesbian or bisexual: Melissa Etheridge, Janis Ian, Skin of Skunk Anansie, Debbie Smith of Echobelly and Horse.

But, at the time of writing, Britain has no out lesbian MPs; there are no out lesbian cabinet ministers on either side of the Atlantic. No Hollywood or major TV star has dared risk their status by being honest. As the millennium beckons, these bald facts undermine all the gains that have been made in the late 20th century. And, of course, this makes it harder yet for all those teachers, nurses, waitresses, doctors, mothers, sisters and daughters who, despite having more than 2,500 years of history to point to, still live in a world which, for the most part, don't even like the word 'lesbian', never mind the women behind the word.

Skin

You doubt it? Then look at the way history can repeat itself: In September 1991, 18-year-old Jennifer Saunders was found guilty of two charges of indecently assaulting two other women and sentenced to six years' imprisonment. Justice Jonathan Crabtree said, 'I suspect these girls would rather have been raped by some young man than have happen to them what you did'. Justifying the heavy sentence, he continued, 'In these days of openness about lesbian and bisexual behaviour it will ensure that anybody else who is tempted to try and copy what you do will count the cost'. And what was Saunders' crime? When she was 16, she had two affairs with other young women. In order to conceal their sexuality from their parents, she agreed to pretend to be a young man, calling herself 'Jimmy'. At her trial, Jennifer Saunders found herself in the same position as Catherina Linck in Germany, 250 years earlier - hearing her former lovers swearing on oath that they had no idea that she was a woman.

Notes

Notes

Published by MQ Publications Ltd
254-258 Goswell Road, London EC1V 7EB

ISBN: 1-897954-92-1

Printed and bound in Hong Kong